Scholastic Success With Tests:
Math Workbook

Grade 6

by Michael Priestley

SCHOLASTIC
PROFESSIONAL BOOKS

New York • Toronto • London • Auckland • Sydney •
Mexico City • New Delhi • Hong Kong • Buenos Aires

No part of this publication may be reproduced in whole or in part, or stored in a retrieval system, or transmitted in any form or by any means electronic, mechanical, photocopying, recording or otherwise, without written permission of the publisher. For information regarding permission, write to Scholastic Inc., 524 Broadway, New York, NY 10012.

Cover design by Maria Lilja
Cover art by Victoria Raymond
Interior design by Creative Pages Inc.
Interior illustrations by Kate Flanagan

ISBN 0-439-42570-0

2 3 4 5 6 7 8 9 10   40   08 07 06 05 04 03

Contents

Introduction

In this book, you will find eight Practice Tests designed to help students prepare to take standardized tests. Each test has 20–30 multiple-choice items that closely resemble the kinds of questions students will have to answer on "real" tests. Each part of the test will take 30–40 minutes for students to complete.

The Math skills measured in these tests and the types of questions are based on detailed analyses and correlations of the five most widely used standardized tests and the curriculum standards measured by many statewide tests, including the following:

Stanford Achievement Test   California's STAR Test
CTBS TerraNova   TAAS (Texas)
Metropolitan Achievement Test   MCAS (Massachusetts)
Iowa Test of Basic Skills   FCAT (Florida)
California Achievement Test   New York

How to Use the Tests

Tell students how much time they will have to complete the test. Encourage students to work quickly and carefully and to keep track of the remaining time—just as they would in a real testing session. You may have students mark their answers directly on the test pages, or you may have them use a copy of the **Answer Sheet**. A copy of the answer sheet appears at the end of each test. The answer sheet will help students become accustomed to filling in bubbles on a real test. It may also make the tests easier for you to score.

We do not recommend the use of calculators. For Practice Tests 2 and 6, students will need an inch ruler and a centimeter ruler to answer some of the questions.

At the back of this book, you will find **Tested Skills** charts and **Answer Keys** for the eight Practice Tests. The Tested Skills charts list the skills measured in each test and the test questions that measure each skill. These charts may be helpful to you in determining what kinds of questions students answered incorrectly, what skills they may be having trouble with, and who may need further instruction in particular skills. To score a Practice Test, refer to the Answer Key for that test. The Answer Key lists the correct response to each question.

To score a Practice Test, go through the test and mark each question answered correctly. Add the total number of questions answered correctly to find the student's test score. To find a percentage score, divide the number answered correctly by the total number of questions. For example, the percentage score for a student who answers 20 out of 25 questions correctly is $20 \div 25 = 0.80$, or 80%. You might want to have students correct their own tests. This will give them a chance to see where they made mistakes and what they need to do to improve their scores on the next test.

On the next page of this book, you will find **Test-Taking Tips**. You may want to share these tips and strategies with students before they begin working on the Practice Tests.

Test-Taking Tips: Mathematics

1. For each part of the test, read the directions carefully so you know what to do. Then read the directions again—just to make sure.

2. Look for key words and phrases to help you decide what each question is asking and what kind of computation you need to do. Examples of key words: *less than, greatest, least, farther, longest, divided equally.*

3. To help solve a problem, write a number sentence or equation.

4. Use scrap paper (or extra space on the test page) to write down the numbers and information you need to solve a problem.

5. If a question has a picture or diagram, study it carefully. Draw your own picture or diagram if it will help you solve a problem.

6. Try to solve each problem before you look at the answer choices. (In some tests, the correct answer may be "Not Given" or "Not Here," so you will want to be sure of your answer. In these Practice Tests, some of the Math questions use "NG" for "Not Given.")

7. Check your work carefully before you finish. (In many questions, you can check your answer by working backwards to see if the numbers work out correctly.)

8. If you are not sure which answer is correct, cross out every answer that you know is wrong. Then make your best guess.

9. To complete a number sentence or equation, try all the answer choices until you find the one that works.

10. When working with fractions, always reduce (or rename) the fractions to their lowest parts. When working with decimals, keep the decimal points lined up correctly.

Practice
Test 1

Numeration and
Number Concepts

Practice Test 1

Directions. Choose the best answer to each question. Mark your answer.

1. The population of Phoenix, Arizona, was 1,198,064. How should this number be written in words?

   (A) one million nineteen thousand eight hundred sixty-four

   (B) one million one hundred ninety-eight thousand sixty-four

   (C) one million one hundred ninety-eight thousand six hundred forty

   (D) one billion one hundred ninety-eight million sixty-four

2. In 1999, a total of four million seven hundred thousand people visited Seaworld Florida. How should that be written in numerals?

   (F) 4,000,700

   (G) 4,070,000

   (H) 4,700,000

   (J) 4,007,000

3. The chart lists the population of four African countries.

Country	Population
Malawi	10,385,849
Mali	10,685,948
Mozambique	19,104,696
Niger	10,075,511

   Which country has the smallest population?

   (A) Malawi

   (B) Mali

   (C) Mozambique

   (D) Niger

4. The chart shows the leading money winners in ladies' golf from 1992 to 1995.

Year	Player	Earnings
1992	Dottie Mochrie	$693,335
1993	Betsy King	$595,992
1994	Laura Davies	$687,201
1995	Annika Sorenstam	$666,533

   Which list shows the players in order from most money to least money earned?

   (F) Mochrie, Davies, Sorenstam, King

   (G) Sorenstam, Davies, Mochrie, King

   (H) Davies, Mochrie, Sorenstam, King

   (J) King, Sorenstam, Davies, Mochrie

GO ON

Practice Test 1 (continued)

5. This chart shows the average winter temperature over four days.

Day	Average Temperature
Sunday	−12°F
Monday	0°F
Tuesday	−4°F
Wednesday	6°F

Which day had the lowest average temperature?
- (A) Sunday
- (B) Monday
- (C) Tuesday
- (D) Wednesday

6. The planet Mercury is about 35,980,000 miles from the sun. What is the value of the **5** in 35,980,000?
- (F) 5 million
- (G) 5 hundred thousand
- (H) 5 thousand
- (J) 5 hundred

7. Which is an odd number?
- (A) 2390
- (B) 7702
- (C) 3475
- (D) 4806

8. The diameter of Jupiter is about 86,882 miles. What is that number rounded to the nearest thousand?
- (F) 87,800
- (G) 87,000
- (H) 86,900
- (J) 86,000

9. There are about 1,265,000,000 people in China. What place value is represented by the **1** in **1,265,000,000**?
- (A) hundred millions
- (B) hundred thousands
- (C) millions
- (D) billions

10. 4,000,000 + 30,000 + 8000 + 20 =
- (F) 4,380,020
- (G) 4,308,200
- (H) 4,038,020
- (J) 4,030,820

Practice Test 1 (continued)

11. $3.4 \times 10^2 =$

Ⓐ 304
Ⓑ 340
Ⓒ 3400
Ⓓ 34,000

12. $5^4 =$

Ⓕ 5×4
Ⓖ $5 \times 5 \times 4$
Ⓗ $5 \times 4 \times 5 \times 4$
Ⓙ $5 \times 5 \times 5 \times 5$

13. Janice created this number pattern.

2, 5, 11, 23, ____

If this pattern continues, what number should come next?

Ⓐ 24
Ⓑ 46
Ⓒ 47
Ⓓ 48

14. Greg made this pattern with tiles.

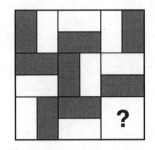

Which square fits in the empty space to complete the pattern?

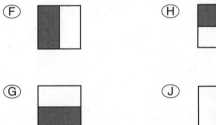

Ⓕ   Ⓗ

Ⓖ   Ⓙ

15. Which is a prime number?

Ⓐ 9
Ⓑ 10
Ⓒ 14
Ⓓ 17

16. Which numbers are both factors of 39?

Ⓕ 6, 7
Ⓖ 3, 13
Ⓗ 5, 8
Ⓙ 4, 9

GO ON

Practice Test 1 (continued)

17. What is the least common multiple of
4, 5, and 10?

Ⓐ 10

Ⓑ 20

Ⓒ 40

Ⓓ 50

18. The Acme Trucking Company has
three vans. Last year, Van A was driven
24,725 miles. Van B was driven 19,620
miles. Van C was driven 30,480 miles.
About how many miles did the three vans
travel all together?

Ⓕ 40,000 miles

Ⓖ 60,000 miles

Ⓗ 75,000 miles

Ⓙ 100,000 miles

19. A stadium in Michigan holds 104,895
people. A stadium in Alabama holds
85,107 people. **About** how many more
people does the Michigan stadium hold?

Ⓐ 20,000

Ⓑ 15,000

Ⓒ 10,000

Ⓓ 5000

20. Look at the number line.

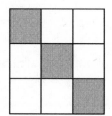

-300   -200   -100   0   100   200   300

The arrow is pointing to what number
on the number line?

Ⓕ −160

Ⓖ −140

Ⓗ −120

Ⓙ −40

21. What fractional part of the figure
is shaded?

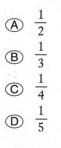

Ⓐ $\frac{1}{2}$

Ⓑ $\frac{1}{3}$

Ⓒ $\frac{1}{4}$

Ⓓ $\frac{1}{5}$

22. Of the 120 cars in a parking lot, 24 are
blue. What fractional part of the cars in
the lot are blue?

Ⓕ $\frac{1}{5}$

Ⓖ $\frac{1}{3}$

Ⓗ $\frac{1}{4}$

Ⓙ $\frac{1}{6}$

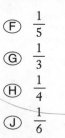

GO ON

Practice Test 1 *(continued)*

23. The chart shows the length of the winning triple jump in four Summer Olympics.

Year	Athlete	Length
1988	K. Markov	17.61 m
1992	M. Conley	18.17 m
1996	K. Harrison	18.09 m
2000	J. Edwards	17.71 m

Who had the longest triple jump?
Ⓐ K. Markov
Ⓑ M. Conley
Ⓒ K. Harrison
Ⓓ J. Edwards

24. Look at the number line.

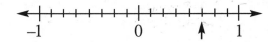

The arrow is pointing to what number on the number line?
Ⓕ $\frac{1}{2}$
Ⓖ $\frac{2}{3}$
Ⓗ $\frac{5}{8}$
Ⓙ $\frac{3}{8}$

25. Which is the *least* amount?
Ⓐ $\frac{1}{4}$ cup
Ⓑ $\frac{1}{3}$ cup
Ⓒ $\frac{1}{6}$ cup
Ⓓ $\frac{1}{8}$ cup

26. Which fraction is another name for $3\frac{1}{2}$?
Ⓕ $\frac{7}{2}$
Ⓖ $\frac{4}{2}$
Ⓗ $\frac{5}{2}$
Ⓙ $\frac{6}{2}$

27. $\frac{45}{100} =$

Ⓐ 4.5
Ⓑ 4.05
Ⓒ 0.45
Ⓓ 0.045

28. Which number sentence is true?
Ⓕ $1 + \frac{1}{2} = \frac{2}{2}$
Ⓖ $\frac{1}{2} \times 0 = 0$
Ⓗ $\frac{3}{4} \times 1 = 1$
Ⓙ $\frac{1}{2} \times \frac{3}{4} = \frac{1}{4} \times \frac{2}{3}$

STOP

ANSWER SHEET

Practice Test # 1

Student Name _____ Grade _____

Teacher Name _____ Date _____

MATHEMATICS

1 Ⓐ Ⓑ Ⓒ Ⓓ Ⓔ	**11** Ⓐ Ⓑ Ⓒ Ⓓ Ⓔ	**21** Ⓐ Ⓑ Ⓒ Ⓓ Ⓔ	**31** Ⓐ Ⓑ Ⓒ Ⓓ Ⓔ
2 Ⓕ Ⓖ Ⓗ Ⓙ Ⓚ	**12** Ⓕ Ⓖ Ⓗ Ⓙ Ⓚ	**22** Ⓕ Ⓖ Ⓗ Ⓙ Ⓚ	**32** Ⓕ Ⓖ Ⓗ Ⓙ Ⓚ
3 Ⓐ Ⓑ Ⓒ Ⓓ Ⓔ	**13** Ⓐ Ⓑ Ⓒ Ⓓ Ⓔ	**23** Ⓐ Ⓑ Ⓒ Ⓓ Ⓔ	**33** Ⓐ Ⓑ Ⓒ Ⓓ Ⓔ
4 Ⓕ Ⓖ Ⓗ Ⓙ Ⓚ	**14** Ⓕ Ⓖ Ⓗ Ⓙ Ⓚ	**24** Ⓕ Ⓖ Ⓗ Ⓙ Ⓚ	**34** Ⓕ Ⓖ Ⓗ Ⓙ Ⓚ
5 Ⓐ Ⓑ Ⓒ Ⓓ Ⓔ	**15** Ⓐ Ⓑ Ⓒ Ⓓ Ⓔ	**25** Ⓐ Ⓑ Ⓒ Ⓓ Ⓔ	**35** Ⓐ Ⓑ Ⓒ Ⓓ Ⓔ
6 Ⓕ Ⓖ Ⓗ Ⓙ Ⓚ	**16** Ⓕ Ⓖ Ⓗ Ⓙ Ⓚ	**26** Ⓕ Ⓖ Ⓗ Ⓙ Ⓚ	**36** Ⓕ Ⓖ Ⓗ Ⓙ Ⓚ
7 Ⓐ Ⓑ Ⓒ Ⓓ Ⓔ	**17** Ⓐ Ⓑ Ⓒ Ⓓ Ⓔ	**27** Ⓐ Ⓑ Ⓒ Ⓓ Ⓔ	**37** Ⓐ Ⓑ Ⓒ Ⓓ Ⓔ
8 Ⓕ Ⓖ Ⓗ Ⓙ Ⓚ	**18** Ⓕ Ⓖ Ⓗ Ⓙ Ⓚ	**28** Ⓕ Ⓖ Ⓗ Ⓙ Ⓚ	**38** Ⓕ Ⓖ Ⓗ Ⓙ Ⓚ
9 Ⓐ Ⓑ Ⓒ Ⓓ Ⓔ	**19** Ⓐ Ⓑ Ⓒ Ⓓ Ⓔ	**29** Ⓐ Ⓑ Ⓒ Ⓓ Ⓔ	**39** Ⓐ Ⓑ Ⓒ Ⓓ Ⓔ
10 Ⓕ Ⓖ Ⓗ Ⓙ Ⓚ	**20** Ⓕ Ⓖ Ⓗ Ⓙ Ⓚ	**30** Ⓕ Ⓖ Ⓗ Ⓙ Ⓚ	**40** Ⓕ Ⓖ Ⓗ Ⓙ Ⓚ

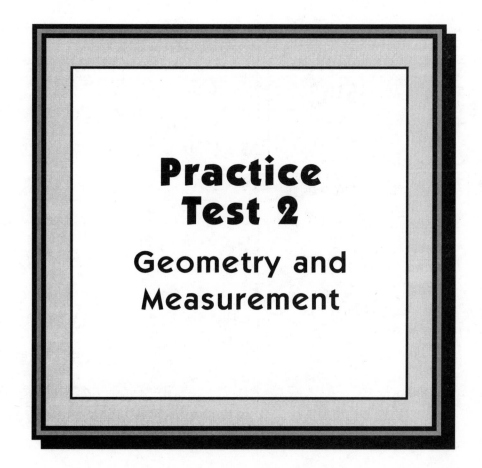

Practice
Test 2

Geometry and
Measurement

Practice Test 2

Directions. Choose the best answer to each question. Mark your answer.

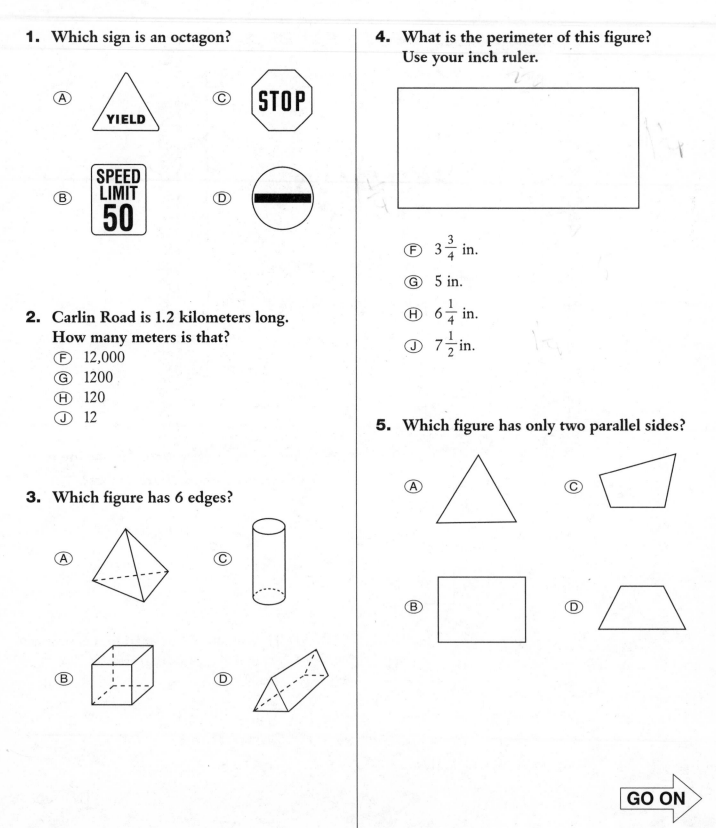

1. Which sign is an octagon?

Ⓐ YIELD

Ⓒ STOP

Ⓑ SPEED LIMIT 50

Ⓓ

2. Carlin Road is 1.2 kilometers long. How many meters is that?

Ⓕ 12,000

Ⓖ 1200

Ⓗ 120

Ⓙ 12

3. Which figure has 6 edges?

Ⓐ

Ⓒ

Ⓑ

Ⓓ

4. What is the perimeter of this figure? Use your inch ruler.

Ⓕ $3\frac{3}{4}$ in.

Ⓖ 5 in.

Ⓗ $6\frac{1}{4}$ in.

Ⓙ $7\frac{1}{2}$ in.

5. Which figure has only two parallel sides?

Ⓐ

Ⓒ

Ⓑ

Ⓓ

GO ON ▷

Practice Test 2 *(continued)*

6. Point O is at the center of this circle. Which line segment is a radius of the circle?

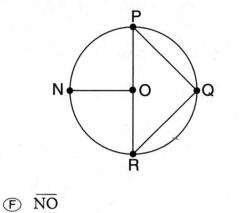

- Ⓕ $\overline{NO}$
- Ⓖ $\overline{QR}$
- Ⓗ $\overline{PQ}$
- Ⓙ $\overline{PR}$

7. Which figure shows a line of symmetry?

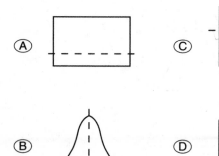

8. Which figure is congruent to Figure A?

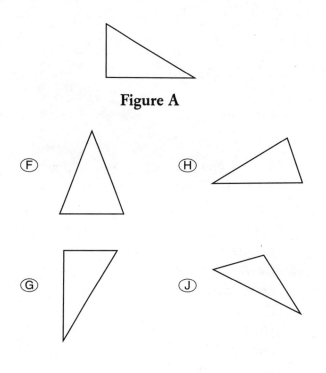

Figure A

9. Mr. Kelly put $8\frac{1}{2}$ gallons of gasoline in his car. How many quarts is that?

- Ⓐ 17 qt
- Ⓑ 24 qt
- Ⓒ 32 qt
- Ⓓ 34 qt

10. Which unit should be used to measure the weight of a bag of potato chips?

- Ⓕ pounds
- Ⓖ cups
- Ⓗ ounces
- Ⓙ inches

GO ON

Practice Test 2 (continued)

11. In this rectangular figure, what is the area of the shaded part?

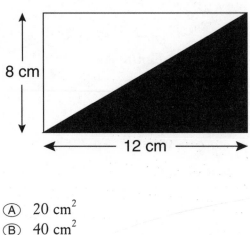

8 cm

12 cm

Ⓐ 20 cm²

Ⓑ 40 cm²

Ⓒ 48 cm²

Ⓓ 96 cm²

12. A pilot flew 1950 miles on Monday, 2110 miles on Tuesday, and 984 miles on Wednesday. About how many miles did she fly in all?

Ⓕ 3000

Ⓖ 4000

Ⓗ 5000

Ⓙ 6000

13. A paving stone weighs $9\frac{3}{4}$ pounds. About how much do 32 paving stones weigh?

Ⓐ 200 lb

Ⓑ 300 lb

Ⓒ 400 lb

Ⓓ 500 lb

The graph below shows the outside temperature recorded at different times on December 12. Use the graph to answer questions 14 and 15.

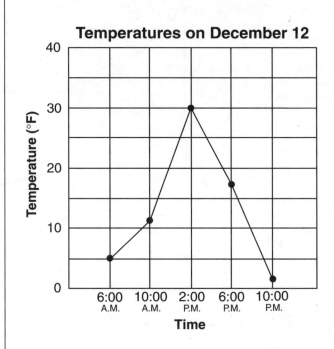

Temperatures on December 12

14. What was the temperature at 2:00 P.M.?

Ⓕ 12°F

Ⓖ 18°F

Ⓗ 20°F

Ⓙ 30°F

15. The lowest temperature was recorded at what time?

Ⓐ 6:00 A.M.

Ⓑ 10:00 A.M.

Ⓒ 6:00 P.M.

Ⓓ 10:00 P.M.

GO ON

Practice Test 2 *(continued)*

16. About how much does a bag of potatoes weigh?

   (F) 10 pounds

   (G) 10 ounces

   (H) 10 grams

   (J) 10 tons

Use the figure below to answer questions 17 and 18.

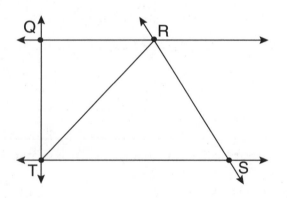

17. Which is perpendicular to QR?

   (A) $\overline{RT}$

   (B) $\overleftrightarrow{RS}$

   (C) $\overleftrightarrow{TS}$

   (D) $\overleftrightarrow{QT}$

18. Which angle is greater than 90 degrees?

   (F) ∠QTS

   (G) ∠QRS

   (H) ∠TSR

   (J) ∠TRS

Use this map and an inch ruler to answer questions 19 and 20.

Blue Lake State Park

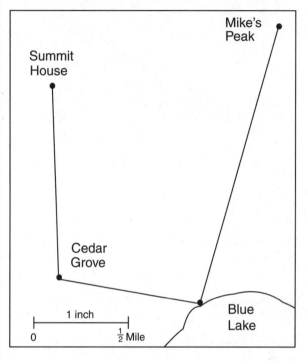

19. What is the actual distance from Summit House to Cedar Grove?

   (A) $\frac{1}{2}$ mile

   (C) $1\frac{1}{2}$ miles

   (B) 1 mile

   (D) 2 miles

20. Deanne hiked from Cedar Grove to Blue Lake and then to Mike's Peak. How far did she hike in all?

   (F) $\frac{3}{4}$ mile

   (H) 2 miles

   (G) $1\frac{1}{2}$ miles

   (J) $2\frac{1}{4}$ miles

GO ON

Practice Test 2 (continued)

21. What is the volume of this figure?

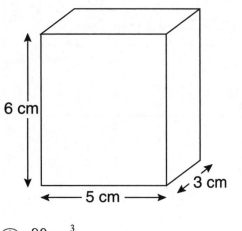

- Ⓐ 90 cm³
- Ⓑ 48 cm³
- Ⓒ 33 cm³
- Ⓓ 14 cm³

22. This figure will be flipped over the line *x*.

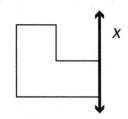

What will the figure look like after it has been flipped?

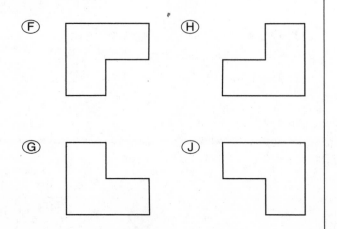

This graph shows the kinds of movies available at the Spotlight Video store. Use the graph to answer questions 23 and 24.

23. Spotlight Video has a total of 1000 movies. About how many are Adventure movies?
- Ⓐ 100
- Ⓑ 250
- Ⓒ 500
- Ⓓ 800

24. Which category has the most movies?
- Ⓕ Sports
- Ⓖ Comedy
- Ⓗ Children's
- Ⓙ Drama

Scholastic Professional Books

ANSWER SHEET

Student Name _____ Grade _____

Teacher Name _____ Date _____

MATHEMATICS

1 ⒶⒷⒸⒹⒺ	11 ⒶⒷⒸⒹⒺ	21 ⒶⒷⒸⒹⒺ	31 ⒶⒷⒸⒹⒺ
2 ⒻⒼⒽⒿⓀ	12 ⒻⒼⒽⒿⓀ	22 ⒻⒼⒽⒿⓀ	32 ⒻⒼⒽⒿⓀ
3 ⒶⒷⒸⒹⒺ	13 ⒶⒷⒸⒹⒺ	23 ⒶⒷⒸⒹⒺ	33 ⒶⒷⒸⒹⒺ
4 ⒻⒼⒽⒿⓀ	14 ⒻⒼⒽⒿⓀ	24 ⒻⒼⒽⒿⓀ	34 ⒻⒼⒽⒿⓀ
5 ⒶⒷⒸⒹⒺ	15 ⒶⒷⒸⒹⒺ	25 ⒶⒷⒸⒹⒺ	35 ⒶⒷⒸⒹⒺ
6 ⒻⒼⒽⒿⓀ	16 ⒻⒼⒽⒿⓀ	26 ⒻⒼⒽⒿⓀ	36 ⒻⒼⒽⒿⓀ
7 ⒶⒷⒸⒹⒺ	17 ⒶⒷⒸⒹⒺ	27 ⒶⒷⒸⒹⒺ	37 ⒶⒷⒸⒹⒺ
8 ⒻⒼⒽⒿⓀ	18 ⒻⒼⒽⒿⓀ	28 ⒻⒼⒽⒿⓀ	38 ⒻⒼⒽⒿⓀ
9 ⒶⒷⒸⒹⒺ	19 ⒶⒷⒸⒹⒺ	29 ⒶⒷⒸⒹⒺ	39 ⒶⒷⒸⒹⒺ
10 ⒻⒼⒽⒿⓀ	20 ⒻⒼⒽⒿⓀ	30 ⒻⒼⒽⒿⓀ	40 ⒻⒼⒽⒿⓀ

Practice
Test 3
Problem Solving

Practice Test 3

Directions. Choose the best answer to each question. Mark your answer. If the correct answer is *not given,* choose "NG."

1. A farmer made $1\frac{3}{4}$ pounds of goat cheese and $2\frac{1}{8}$ pounds of cheddar cheese. How much cheese did she make in all?

   Ⓐ $3\frac{4}{12}$ lb

   Ⓑ $3\frac{7}{8}$ lb

   Ⓒ $3\frac{1}{2}$ lb

   Ⓓ $3\frac{1}{4}$ lb

   Ⓔ NG

2. Shari bought these 3 books.

   What is the total cost of these books?
   Ⓕ $48.70
   Ⓖ $53.55
   Ⓗ $63.55
   Ⓙ $63.65
   Ⓚ NG

3. A parking garage has 12 rows of parking spaces with 14 spaces in each row. How many cars can park in the garage at one time?
   Ⓐ 26
   Ⓑ 144
   Ⓒ 168
   Ⓓ 196
   Ⓔ NG

4. Leon needs $82.00 for a new skateboard. He has saved $41.00. What percent of the total amount has he saved?
   Ⓕ 60%
   Ⓖ 50%
   Ⓗ 41%
   Ⓙ 30%
   Ⓚ NG

5. A pair of socks costs $4.95. A package of 3 pairs costs $12.00.

   $4.95   **$12.00**

   How much do you save on 3 pairs of socks if you buy the package?
   Ⓐ $2.85
   Ⓑ $3.10
   Ⓒ $9.90
   Ⓓ $14.85
   Ⓔ NG

6. The owner of a mini-golf park bought 2 boxes of golf balls in June. Each box had 150 golf balls. By the end of August, players had lost 62 golf balls. How many were left?
   Ⓕ 88
   Ⓖ 90
   Ⓗ 238
   Ⓙ 362
   Ⓚ NG

GO ON ⇨

Scholastic Professional Books

Practice Test 3 *(continued)*

7. Maureen wants to buy a winter coat that usually costs $50.00. The coat is on sale.

What is the sale price of the coat?

Ⓐ $15.00
Ⓑ $30.00
Ⓒ $35.00
Ⓓ $47.00
Ⓔ NG

8. Justin was playing a game on his computer. He started playing at 1:15 P.M. and stopped playing at 3:40 P.M. How long did he play the game?

Ⓕ 2 hr 15 min
Ⓖ 2 hr 20 min
Ⓗ 2 hr 35 min
Ⓙ 3 hr 5 min
Ⓚ NG

9. Mrs. Klein uses 12 cucumbers to make 3 jars of pickles. At this rate, how many cucumbers will she need to make 10 jars of pickles?

Ⓐ 24
Ⓑ 30
Ⓒ 32
Ⓓ 40
Ⓔ NG

10. Candy bought a box of 50 books at a used book sale. Of those books, $\frac{3}{5}$ were paperbacks. How many paperback books did she buy?

Ⓕ 20
Ⓖ 25
Ⓗ 30
Ⓙ 35
Ⓚ NG

11. Tori made 2 gallons of lemonade. There are 16 cups in a gallon. If she sells all the lemonade for $0.50 a cup, how much money will she make?

Ⓐ $32.00
Ⓑ $20.00
Ⓒ $12.00
Ⓓ $10.00
Ⓔ NG

Scholastic Professional Books

Practice Test 3 (continued)

12. Five students sat in a row of seats in the auditorium. Bruce sat on one end. Grace sat between Bruce and Miles. Rita sat between Miles and Chad.

Who sat in the middle seat?

Ⓕ Rita
Ⓖ Grace
Ⓗ Chad
Ⓙ Miles
Ⓚ NG

13. There are 98 boxes of seats at the football stadium. Each box has 12 seats. Which numbers would give the best estimate of the total number of box seats in the stadium?

Ⓐ 90 × 10
Ⓑ 90 × 20
Ⓒ 100 × 10
Ⓓ 100 × 20

14. Steve earns $7.85 per hour at a fast food restaurant. About how much will he make in 42 hours?

Ⓕ $400
Ⓖ $360
Ⓗ $320
Ⓙ $280

15. Mr. Guerrero gets 22 miles per gallon of gasoline in his truck. About how many miles can he go on 28 gallons of gasoline?

Ⓐ 400
Ⓑ 600
Ⓒ 800
Ⓓ 1000

16. Casey read a book in 5 days. She read 30 pages on the first day and 50 pages on the last day. What else do you need to know to find the average number of pages she read each day?

Ⓕ the total number of pages in the book
Ⓖ how many hours she read each day
Ⓗ on which days of the week she read
Ⓙ the number of books she reads each year

Practice Test 3 *(continued)*

17. Mario baby-sat for a total of 28 hours last week. He earns $6.00 per hour for baby-sitting. Which question can you answer from this information?

  Ⓐ How many different families did Mario baby-sit for?

  Ⓑ What is the average amount of money Mario earns each week?

  Ⓒ How many children did Mario baby-sit during the week?

  Ⓓ How much money did Mario earn last week for baby-sitting?

  Ⓔ NG

18. At a toy factory, workers pack 32 toys in a box for shipping. Which number sentence should you use to find how many boxes they will need to pack 2048 toys?

  Ⓕ $2048 - 32 = \square$

  Ⓖ $2048 \div 32 = \square$

  Ⓗ $2048 \times 32 = \square$

  Ⓙ $2048 + 32 = \square$

  Ⓚ NG

19. Mrs. Bryant counted 25 birds at her bird feeder one morning. Of those birds, 10 were blue jays. What percent of the birds were blue jays?

  Ⓐ 10%

  Ⓑ 25%

  Ⓒ 30%

  Ⓓ 45%

  Ⓔ NG

20. Duncan was baking bread and cakes for a bake sale. He used $5\frac{1}{4}$ cups of flour for bread and $6\frac{3}{8}$ cups of flour for cakes.

$5\frac{1}{4}$ cups

$6\frac{3}{8}$ cups

How much flour did he use in all?

  Ⓕ $11\frac{4}{12}$ cups

  Ⓖ $11\frac{1}{2}$ cups

  Ⓗ $11\frac{5}{8}$ cups

  Ⓙ $12\frac{1}{8}$ cups

  Ⓚ NG

GO ON

Practice Test 3 *(continued)*

21. Mr. Chasse bought 4 tires at a tire sale.

TIRE SALE
$112.50 each

Including a sales tax of 6%, what was the total cost for the 4 tires?

- (A) $477.00
- (B) $474.00
- (C) $456.00
- (D) $450.00
- (E) NG

22. Three buses were used for a field trip to the Science Center. There were 32 students on each bus. Tickets for the Science Center cost $7.50 each.

32   32   32

Science Center
$7.50

What was the cost of the tickets for all the students on the field trip?

- (F) $240.00
- (G) $480.00
- (H) $610.00
- (J) $720.00
- (K) NG

23. On average, 162 cars go through the Coolidge Tunnel each hour. How many cars go through the tunnel in 12 hours?

- (A) 174
- (B) 486
- (C) 1944
- (D) 2044
- (E) NG

24. A baker can fill 12 jelly donuts in $1\frac{1}{2}$ minutes. At this rate, how long will it take her to fill 48 donuts?

- (F) 4 minutes
- (G) $5\frac{1}{2}$ minutes
- (H) $6\frac{1}{2}$ minutes
- (J) 8 minutes
- (K) NG

25. In a ski race, Adele finished in 38.75 seconds. Graham's time was 39.09 seconds. How much faster was Adele's time in the race?

- (A) 0.25 seconds
- (B) 0.34 seconds
- (C) 0.84 seconds
- (D) 1.66 seconds
- (E) NG

STOP

ANSWER SHEET

Practice Test # 3

Student Name _____ Grade _____

Teacher Name _____ Date _____

MATHEMATICS

1 Ⓐ Ⓑ Ⓒ Ⓓ Ⓔ 11 Ⓐ Ⓑ Ⓒ Ⓓ Ⓔ 21 Ⓐ Ⓑ Ⓒ Ⓓ Ⓔ 31 Ⓐ Ⓑ Ⓒ Ⓓ Ⓔ

2 Ⓕ Ⓖ Ⓗ Ⓙ Ⓚ 12 Ⓕ Ⓖ Ⓗ Ⓙ Ⓚ 22 Ⓕ Ⓖ Ⓗ Ⓙ Ⓚ 32 Ⓕ Ⓖ Ⓗ Ⓙ Ⓚ

3 Ⓐ Ⓑ Ⓒ Ⓓ Ⓔ 13 Ⓐ Ⓑ Ⓒ Ⓓ Ⓔ 23 Ⓐ Ⓑ Ⓒ Ⓓ Ⓔ 33 Ⓐ Ⓑ Ⓒ Ⓓ Ⓔ

4 Ⓕ Ⓖ Ⓗ Ⓙ Ⓚ 14 Ⓕ Ⓖ Ⓗ Ⓙ Ⓚ 24 Ⓕ Ⓖ Ⓗ Ⓙ Ⓚ 34 Ⓕ Ⓖ Ⓗ Ⓙ Ⓚ

5 Ⓐ Ⓑ Ⓒ Ⓓ Ⓔ 15 Ⓐ Ⓑ Ⓒ Ⓓ Ⓔ 25 Ⓐ Ⓑ Ⓒ Ⓓ Ⓔ 35 Ⓐ Ⓑ Ⓒ Ⓓ Ⓔ

6 Ⓕ Ⓖ Ⓗ Ⓙ Ⓚ 16 Ⓕ Ⓖ Ⓗ Ⓙ Ⓚ 26 Ⓕ Ⓖ Ⓗ Ⓙ Ⓚ 36 Ⓕ Ⓖ Ⓗ Ⓙ Ⓚ

7 Ⓐ Ⓑ Ⓒ Ⓓ Ⓔ 17 Ⓐ Ⓑ Ⓒ Ⓓ Ⓔ 27 Ⓐ Ⓑ Ⓒ Ⓓ Ⓔ 37 Ⓐ Ⓑ Ⓒ Ⓓ Ⓔ

8 Ⓕ Ⓖ Ⓗ Ⓙ Ⓚ 18 Ⓕ Ⓖ Ⓗ Ⓙ Ⓚ 28 Ⓕ Ⓖ Ⓗ Ⓙ Ⓚ 38 Ⓕ Ⓖ Ⓗ Ⓙ Ⓚ

9 Ⓐ Ⓑ Ⓒ Ⓓ Ⓔ 19 Ⓐ Ⓑ Ⓒ Ⓓ Ⓔ 29 Ⓐ Ⓑ Ⓒ Ⓓ Ⓔ 39 Ⓐ Ⓑ Ⓒ Ⓓ Ⓔ

10 Ⓕ Ⓖ Ⓗ Ⓙ Ⓚ 20 Ⓕ Ⓖ Ⓗ Ⓙ Ⓚ 30 Ⓕ Ⓖ Ⓗ Ⓙ Ⓚ 40 Ⓕ Ⓖ Ⓗ Ⓙ Ⓚ

Practice Test 4

Computation

Practice Test 4

Directions. Choose the best answer to each question. Mark your answer. If the correct answer is *not given,* choose "NG."

1.
$$\begin{array}{r} 58 \\ \times\, 43 \\ \hline \end{array}$$

    (A) 406
    (B) 2394
    (C) 2494
    (D) 2504
    (E) NG

2.   8)199

    (F) 25
    (G) 24 R7
    (H) 24
    (J) 22 R1
    (K) NG

3.   27)567

    (A) 18
    (B) 19
    (C) 20
    (D) 22
    (E) NG

4. This chart shows how many hours a family spent watching TV each week.

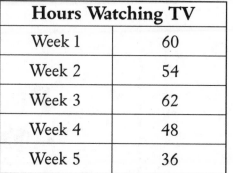

Hours Watching TV	
Week 1	60
Week 2	54
Week 3	62
Week 4	48
Week 5	36

What was the average number of hours spent watching TV per week?
    (F) 36 hours
    (G) 48 hours
    (H) 52 hours
    (J) 260 hours
    (K) NG

5. A jumbo jet can carry 395 passengers.

395

How many passengers can be carried on 4 of these jets?
    (A) 1185
    (B) 1480
    (C) 1560
    (D) 1580
    (E) NG

GO ON

Practice Test 4 (continued)

6. $\frac{1}{5} + \frac{3}{10} =$

    Ⓕ $\frac{1}{2}$

    Ⓖ $\frac{2}{5}$

    Ⓗ $\frac{4}{15}$

    Ⓙ $\frac{7}{10}$

    Ⓚ NG

7. $\frac{2}{3} + \frac{5}{9} =$

    Ⓐ $\frac{7}{9}$

    Ⓑ $\frac{7}{12}$

    Ⓒ $1\frac{1}{9}$

    Ⓓ $1\frac{2}{9}$

    Ⓔ NG

8. $\begin{array}{r} 6\frac{1}{4} \\ -\ \ 3\frac{3}{4} \\ \hline \end{array}$

    Ⓕ 7

    Ⓖ $6\frac{1}{2}$

    Ⓗ $5\frac{1}{4}$

    Ⓙ $5\frac{1}{8}$

    Ⓚ NG

9. $\frac{1}{2} \times \frac{3}{8} =$

    Ⓐ $\frac{1}{4}$

    Ⓑ $\frac{3}{10}$

    Ⓒ $\frac{3}{16}$

    Ⓓ $\frac{2}{5}$

    Ⓔ NG

10. Mary Lee went to a costume shop. She bought 2 old-fashioned hats, 4 coats, and 5 dresses.

Costumes		
Hats 2	Coats 4	Dresses 5

How many different combinations of 1 hat, 1 coat, and 1 dress can she make?

    Ⓕ 11

    Ⓖ 18

    Ⓗ 36

    Ⓙ 40

    Ⓚ NG

11. Stan played the Duck Pond game at the fair. These colored ducks were in the Duck Pond.

Color	Number of Ducks
Yellow	20
White	15
Red	7
Blue	18

If Stan reaches in and takes out one duck without looking, what is the probability that the duck will be white?

    Ⓐ $\frac{1}{3}$

    Ⓑ $\frac{1}{4}$

    Ⓒ $\frac{1}{5}$

    Ⓓ $\frac{1}{6}$

    Ⓔ NG

GO ON ➡

Practice Test 4 (continued)

12. $158.95
      + 42.70

- Ⓕ $191.25
- Ⓖ $191.65
- Ⓗ $200.65
- Ⓙ $201.65
- Ⓚ NG

13. 80.91
      − 26.30

- Ⓐ 107.21
- Ⓑ 66.61
- Ⓒ 64.61
- Ⓓ 52.61
- Ⓔ NG

14. $8 \times 0.6 =$

- Ⓕ 0.48
- Ⓖ 4.8
- Ⓗ 48
- Ⓙ 480
- Ⓚ NG

15. $4\overline{)28.12}$

- Ⓐ 6.03
- Ⓑ 6.93
- Ⓒ 7.03
- Ⓓ 7.3
- Ⓔ NG

Use the graph below to answer questions 16 and 17.

16. Where is point T located?
- Ⓕ (5, 2)
- Ⓖ (2, 1)
- Ⓗ (4, 7)
- Ⓙ (2, 5)
- Ⓚ NG

17. What point is located at (7, 4)?
- Ⓐ point P
- Ⓑ point Q
- Ⓒ point R
- Ⓓ point S
- Ⓔ NG

GO ON

Practice Test 4 (continued)

18. 8% of 50 =

- Ⓕ 2
- Ⓖ 4
- Ⓗ 8
- Ⓙ 40
- Ⓚ NG

19. 70% of $90 =

- Ⓐ $20
- Ⓑ $56
- Ⓒ $65
- Ⓓ $70
- Ⓔ NG

20. 30 is what percent of 40?

- Ⓕ 30%
- Ⓖ 50%
- Ⓗ 60%
- Ⓙ 75%
- Ⓚ NG

21. $-12 + 9 =$

- Ⓐ −3
- Ⓑ 3
- Ⓒ −9
- Ⓓ 21
- Ⓔ NG

22. This table shows the number of children who went to a summer camp each year.

Children at Camp Wahoo	
Year	Number of Children
1998	250
1999	320
2000	300
2001	370

What was the average number of children who went to the camp each year?

- Ⓕ 310
- Ⓖ 320
- Ⓗ 360
- Ⓙ 1240
- Ⓚ NG

23. This table lists the scores Tom got on 5 math tests.

Test	Score
1	75
2	82
3	86
4	64
5	78

What was Tom's median test score?

- Ⓐ 76
- Ⓑ 78
- Ⓒ 80
- Ⓓ 82
- Ⓔ NG

GO ON

Scholastic Professional Books

Practice Test 4 (continued)

24. If $3x - 2 = 10$, what is the value of x?

   Ⓕ 4

   Ⓖ 6

   Ⓗ 8

   Ⓙ 12

   Ⓚ NG

25. If $5n + 5 = 60$, what is the value of n?

   Ⓐ 7

   Ⓑ 9

   Ⓒ 10

   Ⓓ 11

   Ⓔ NG

26. If $7y > 21$, what is the value of y?

   Ⓕ $y < 3$

   Ⓖ $y < 2$

   Ⓗ $y > 3$

   Ⓙ $y > 2$

   Ⓚ NG

27. At 6:00 A.M., the temperature was 50°F. This table shows how much the temperature changed during the day.

Time	Change in Temperature (°F)
8:00 A.M.	+4
12:00 NOON	−2
4:00 P.M.	−10
8:00 P.M.	+3

What was the temperature at 8:00 P.M.?

   Ⓐ 39°F

   Ⓑ 42°F

   Ⓒ 45°F

   Ⓓ 69°F

   Ⓔ NG

28. A shark gained $2\frac{1}{2}$ pounds per day. How much weight did the shark gain in 8 days?

   Ⓕ $10\frac{1}{2}$ lb

   Ⓖ 15 lb

   Ⓗ $17\frac{1}{2}$ lb

   Ⓙ 20 lb

   Ⓚ NG

STOP

ANSWER SHEET

Practice Test # 4

Student Name _____ Grade _____

Teacher Name _____ Date _____

MATHEMATICS

1 Ⓐ Ⓑ Ⓒ Ⓓ Ⓔ	11 Ⓐ Ⓑ Ⓒ Ⓓ Ⓔ	21 Ⓐ Ⓑ Ⓒ Ⓓ Ⓔ	31 Ⓐ Ⓑ Ⓒ Ⓓ Ⓔ
2 Ⓕ Ⓖ Ⓗ Ⓙ Ⓚ	12 Ⓕ Ⓖ Ⓗ Ⓙ Ⓚ	22 Ⓕ Ⓖ Ⓗ Ⓙ Ⓚ	32 Ⓕ Ⓖ Ⓗ Ⓙ Ⓚ
3 Ⓐ Ⓑ Ⓒ Ⓓ Ⓔ	13 Ⓐ Ⓑ Ⓒ Ⓓ Ⓔ	23 Ⓐ Ⓑ Ⓒ Ⓓ Ⓔ	33 Ⓐ Ⓑ Ⓒ Ⓓ Ⓔ
4 Ⓕ Ⓖ Ⓗ Ⓙ Ⓚ	14 Ⓕ Ⓖ Ⓗ Ⓙ Ⓚ	24 Ⓕ Ⓖ Ⓗ Ⓙ Ⓚ	34 Ⓕ Ⓖ Ⓗ Ⓙ Ⓚ
5 Ⓐ Ⓑ Ⓒ Ⓓ Ⓔ	15 Ⓐ Ⓑ Ⓒ Ⓓ Ⓔ	25 Ⓐ Ⓑ Ⓒ Ⓓ Ⓔ	35 Ⓐ Ⓑ Ⓒ Ⓓ Ⓔ
6 Ⓕ Ⓖ Ⓗ Ⓙ Ⓚ	16 Ⓕ Ⓖ Ⓗ Ⓙ Ⓚ	26 Ⓕ Ⓖ Ⓗ Ⓙ Ⓚ	36 Ⓕ Ⓖ Ⓗ Ⓙ Ⓚ
7 Ⓐ Ⓑ Ⓒ Ⓓ Ⓔ	17 Ⓐ Ⓑ Ⓒ Ⓓ Ⓔ	27 Ⓐ Ⓑ Ⓒ Ⓓ Ⓔ	37 Ⓐ Ⓑ Ⓒ Ⓓ Ⓔ
8 Ⓕ Ⓖ Ⓗ Ⓙ Ⓚ	18 Ⓕ Ⓖ Ⓗ Ⓙ Ⓚ	28 Ⓕ Ⓖ Ⓗ Ⓙ Ⓚ	38 Ⓕ Ⓖ Ⓗ Ⓙ Ⓚ
9 Ⓐ Ⓑ Ⓒ Ⓓ Ⓔ	19 Ⓐ Ⓑ Ⓒ Ⓓ Ⓔ	29 Ⓐ Ⓑ Ⓒ Ⓓ Ⓔ	39 Ⓐ Ⓑ Ⓒ Ⓓ Ⓔ
10 Ⓕ Ⓖ Ⓗ Ⓙ Ⓚ	20 Ⓕ Ⓖ Ⓗ Ⓙ Ⓚ	30 Ⓕ Ⓖ Ⓗ Ⓙ Ⓚ	40 Ⓕ Ⓖ Ⓗ Ⓙ Ⓚ

Scholastic Professional Books

Scholastic Success With Tests: Math • Grade 6   33

Practice Test 5

Numeration and Number Concepts

Practice Test 5

Directions. Choose the best answer to each question. Mark your answer.

1. The population of Memphis, Tennessee, was 1,007,306. How should this number be written in words?

Ⓐ one billion seven million three hundred six

Ⓑ one million seven hundred thousand thirty-six

Ⓒ one million seven thousand three hundred six

Ⓓ one million seven thousand three hundred sixty

2. In 1999, a total of five million three hundred seventy thousand fifteen people visited the Statue of Liberty National Monument. How should that be written in numerals?

Ⓕ 5,370,015

Ⓖ 5,307,015

Ⓗ 5,370,150

Ⓙ 5,037,015

3. The chart lists the population of four countries.

Country	Population
Ireland	3,797,257
New Zealand	3,819,762
Norway	4,481,162
Singapore	4,151,720

Which country has the smallest population?

Ⓐ Ireland

Ⓑ New Zealand

Ⓒ Norway

Ⓓ Singapore

4. The chart shows the leading money winners in men's golf from 1990 to 1993.

Year	Player	Earnings
1990	Greg Norman	$1,165,477
1991	Corey Pavin	$979,430
1992	Fred Couples	$1,344,188
1993	Nick Price	$1,478,557

Which list shows the players in order from least money to most money earned?

Ⓕ Price, Couples, Norman, Pavin

Ⓖ Norman, Pavin, Couples, Price

Ⓗ Pavin, Norman, Couples, Price

Ⓙ Pavin, Couples, Price, Norman

GO ON

Practice Test 5 (continued)

5. This chart shows the average temperature on four planets.

Planet	Average Temperature
Mercury	332°F
Venus	67°F
Mars	−82°F
Jupiter	−163°F

Which planet has the lowest average temperature?

Ⓐ Mercury
Ⓑ Venus
Ⓒ Mars
Ⓓ Jupiter

6. The planet Mars is about 154,900,000 miles from the sun. What is the value of the **9** in 154,**9**00,000?

Ⓕ 9 million
Ⓖ 9 hundred thousand
Ⓗ 9 thousand
Ⓙ 9 hundred

7. Which is an odd number?

Ⓐ 1052
Ⓑ 2007
Ⓒ 6240
Ⓓ 8414

8. In 1999, there were 37,992 Blackfoot Indians living in the United States. What is that number rounded to the nearest ten thousand?

Ⓕ 30,000
Ⓖ 37,000
Ⓗ 38,000
Ⓙ 40,000

9. There are about 1,014,003,817 people in India. What place value is represented by the **4** in 1,01**4**,003,817?

Ⓐ hundred millions
Ⓑ hundred thousands
Ⓒ millions
Ⓓ billions

10. 6,000,000 + 500,000 + 1000 + 70 =

Ⓕ 6,501,070
Ⓖ 6,051,070
Ⓗ 6,005,170
Ⓙ 6,510,700

Scholastic Professional Books

Practice Test 5 *(continued)*

11. $7.3 \times 10^3 =$

   Ⓐ 703

   Ⓑ 730

   Ⓒ 7300

   Ⓓ 73,000

12. $4^5 =$

   Ⓕ $4 \times 4 \times 5$

   Ⓖ $4 \times 4 \times 4 \times 4 \times 4$

   Ⓗ $4 \times 5 \times 4 \times 5$

   Ⓙ $4 + 4 + 4 + 4 + 4$

13. Charlotte created this number pattern.

   2, 6, 18, 54, ____

If this pattern continues, what number should come next?

   Ⓐ 55

   Ⓑ 108

   Ⓒ 152

   Ⓓ 162

14. Louis made this pattern with tiles.

Which square fits in the empty space to complete the pattern?

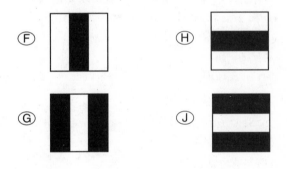

15. Which is a prime number?

   Ⓐ 8

   Ⓑ 9

   Ⓒ 13

   Ⓓ 15

16. Which numbers are both factors of 45?

   Ⓕ 4, 11

   Ⓖ 5, 9

   Ⓗ 6, 7

   Ⓙ 8, 10

GO ON ⟩

Practice Test 5 (continued)

17. What is the least common multiple of 3, 6, and 10?

  Ⓐ 60

  Ⓑ 30

  Ⓒ 18

  Ⓓ 10

18. The Sterling Train Line has been running for three months. In the first month, 18,370 passengers rode the train. There were 22,095 passengers in the second month and 26,810 passengers in the third month. <u>About</u> how many passengers in all rode the train in those three months?

  Ⓕ 48,000

  Ⓖ 67,000

  Ⓗ 75,000

  Ⓙ 90,000

19. In 1999, the population of Utah was 2,129,836. The population of West Virginia was 1,806,928. <u>About</u> how many more people lived in Utah than in West Virginia?

  Ⓐ 30,000

  Ⓑ 200,000

  Ⓒ 300,000

  Ⓓ 400,000

20. Look at the number line.

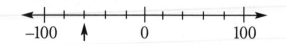

The arrow is pointing to what number on the number line?

  Ⓕ 60

  Ⓖ 80

  Ⓗ −30

  Ⓙ −60

21. What fractional part of the figure is shaded?

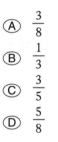

  Ⓐ $\frac{3}{8}$

  Ⓑ $\frac{1}{3}$

  Ⓒ $\frac{3}{5}$

  Ⓓ $\frac{5}{8}$

22. Of the 160 students in a school, 32 have red hair. What fractional part of the students have red hair?

  Ⓕ $\frac{1}{5}$

  Ⓖ $\frac{1}{3}$

  Ⓗ $\frac{1}{4}$

  Ⓙ $\frac{1}{6}$

GO ON ⇨

Practice Test 5 (continued)

23. This chart shows the average price of concert tickets for different performers in 2001.

Performer	Average Ticket Price
'N Sync	$56.61
Sarah Brightman	$57.37
Backstreet Boys	$53.92
Mark Knopfler	$55.02

Which performer had the highest average ticket price?
Ⓐ 'N Sync
Ⓑ Sarah Brightman
Ⓒ Backstreet Boys
Ⓓ Mark Knopfler

24. Look at the number line.

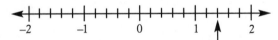

The arrow is pointing to what number on the number line?
Ⓕ $1\frac{1}{2}$
Ⓖ $1\frac{1}{4}$
Ⓗ $1\frac{2}{5}$
Ⓙ $1\frac{2}{3}$

25. Four white mice were weighed for a science experiment. Which mouse weighed *least*?
Ⓐ Mouse A: $1\frac{1}{4}$ ounces
Ⓑ Mouse B: $1\frac{1}{3}$ ounces
Ⓒ Mouse C: $1\frac{1}{5}$ ounces
Ⓓ Mouse D: $1\frac{1}{2}$ ounces

26. Which fraction is another name for $2\frac{1}{4}$?
Ⓕ $\frac{9}{4}$
Ⓖ $\frac{3}{4}$
Ⓗ $\frac{7}{4}$
Ⓙ $\frac{8}{4}$

27. $\frac{65}{100} =$
Ⓐ 0.065
Ⓑ 0.65
Ⓒ 6.5
Ⓓ 65

28. Which number sentence is true?
Ⓕ $3\frac{1}{2} \times 0 = 3\frac{1}{2}$
Ⓖ $\frac{9}{5} \times 1 = 1$
Ⓗ $\frac{1}{7} + \frac{6}{7} = 7$
Ⓙ $\frac{1}{3} \times \frac{2}{7} = \frac{2}{7} \times \frac{1}{3}$

STOP

ANSWER SHEET

Student Name _____ Grade _____

Teacher Name _____ Date _____

MATHEMATICS

1 ⒶⒷⒸⒹⒺ	**11** ⒶⒷⒸⒹⒺ	**21** ⒶⒷⒸⒹⒺ	**31** ⒶⒷⒸⒹⒺ
2 ⒻⒼⒽⒿⓀ	**12** ⒻⒼⒽⒿⓀ	**22** ⒻⒼⒽⒿⓀ	**32** ⒻⒼⒽⒿⓀ
3 ⒶⒷⒸⒹⒺ	**13** ⒶⒷⒸⒹⒺ	**23** ⒶⒷⒸⒹⒺ	**33** ⒶⒷⒸⒹⒺ
4 ⒻⒼⒽⒿⓀ	**14** ⒻⒼⒽⒿⓀ	**24** ⒻⒼⒽⒿⓀ	**34** ⒻⒼⒽⒿⓀ
5 ⒶⒷⒸⒹⒺ	**15** ⒶⒷⒸⒹⒺ	**25** ⒶⒷⒸⒹⒺ	**35** ⒶⒷⒸⒹⒺ
6 ⒻⒼⒽⒿⓀ	**16** ⒻⒼⒽⒿⓀ	**26** ⒻⒼⒽⒿⓀ	**36** ⒻⒼⒽⒿⓀ
7 ⒶⒷⒸⒹⒺ	**17** ⒶⒷⒸⒹⒺ	**27** ⒶⒷⒸⒹⒺ	**37** ⒶⒷⒸⒹⒺ
8 ⒻⒼⒽⒿⓀ	**18** ⒻⒼⒽⒿⓀ	**28** ⒻⒼⒽⒿⓀ	**38** ⒻⒼⒽⒿⓀ
9 ⒶⒷⒸⒹⒺ	**19** ⒶⒷⒸⒹⒺ	**29** ⒶⒷⒸⒹⒺ	**39** ⒶⒷⒸⒹⒺ
10 ⒻⒼⒽⒿⓀ	**20** ⒻⒼⒽⒿⓀ	**30** ⒻⒼⒽⒿⓀ	**40** ⒻⒼⒽⒿⓀ

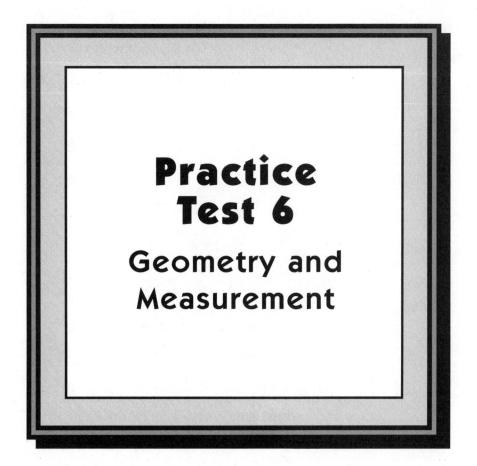

Practice Test 6

Geometry and Measurement

Practice Test 6

Directions. Choose the best answer to each question. Mark your answer.

1. Which figure has 3 faces?

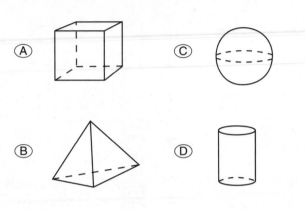

2. A soccer field is 120 yards long. How many feet is that?

- Ⓕ 360
- Ⓖ 240
- Ⓗ 60
- Ⓙ 40

3. Which figure is a trapezoid?

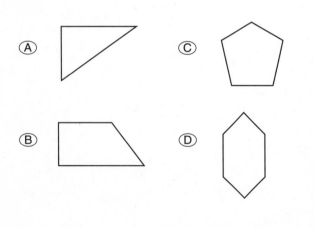

4. What is the perimeter of this figure? Use a centimeter ruler.

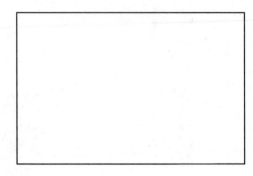

- Ⓕ 10 cm
- Ⓖ 18 cm
- Ⓗ 20 cm
- Ⓙ 24 cm

5. Which figure has no parallel sides?

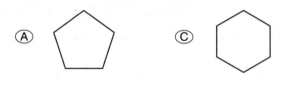

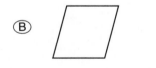

Practice Test 6 *(continued)*

6. Point C is at the center of this circle. Which line segment is the diameter of the circle?

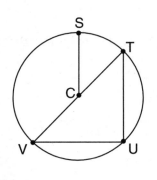

- Ⓕ $\overline{SC}$
- Ⓖ $\overline{TU}$
- Ⓗ $\overline{CV}$
- Ⓙ $\overline{VT}$

7. Which figure is congruent to Figure A?

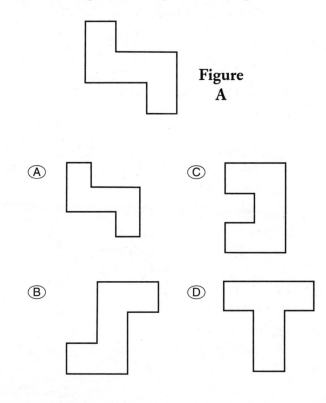

Figure A

- Ⓐ
- Ⓒ
- Ⓑ
- Ⓓ

8. Which name has a line of symmetry?

- Ⓕ DAVE
- Ⓗ TORI
- Ⓖ OTTO
- Ⓙ CHER

9. Mrs. Eames bought a bag of apples with a mass of 4.2 kilograms. How many grams is that?

- Ⓐ 4200
- Ⓑ 420
- Ⓒ 42
- Ⓓ 0.42

10. Which unit should be used to measure the amount of milk in a paper cup?

- Ⓕ pints
- Ⓖ gallons
- Ⓗ ounces
- Ⓙ quarts

GO ON

Practice Test 6 *(continued)*

11. This diagram shows the new deck that Mr. Cohn plans to build.

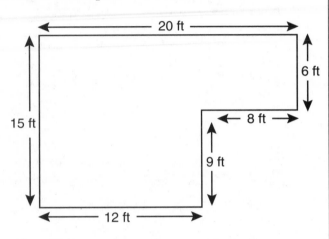

What is the area of the deck?
- Ⓐ 70 sq ft
- Ⓑ 160 sq ft
- Ⓒ 180 sq ft
- Ⓓ 228 sq ft

12. The Big Top circus gave 3 shows. There were 1890 people at the first show, 2015 people at the second show, and 2970 people at the third show. About how many people in all went to the circus?
- Ⓕ 3000
- Ⓖ 5000
- Ⓗ 7000
- Ⓙ 10,000

13. A clay tile weighs $10\frac{1}{4}$ ounces. <u>About</u> how many ounces do 97 tiles weigh?
- Ⓐ 100 oz
- Ⓑ 500 oz
- Ⓒ 1000 oz
- Ⓓ 1500 oz

The graph below shows the top five producers of maple syrup in 2000. Use the graph to answer questions 14 and 15.

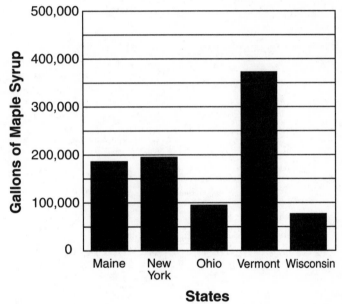

14. Which state produced the most maple syrup?
- Ⓕ Maine
- Ⓖ New York
- Ⓗ Ohio
- Ⓙ Vermont

15. About how much maple syrup did Wisconsin produce?
- Ⓐ 50,000 gal
- Ⓑ 75,000 gal
- Ⓒ 100,000 gal
- Ⓓ 170,000 gal

GO ON ⟩

Practice Test 6 *(continued)*

16. An adult man is most likely to have a mass of —

   Ⓕ 100 milligrams
   Ⓖ 100 grams
   Ⓗ 100 kilograms
   Ⓙ 100 tons

Use the figure below to answer questions 17 and 18.

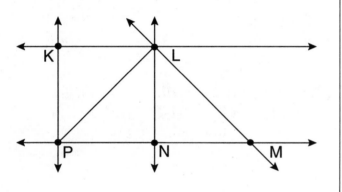

17. Which angle is less than 90 degrees?

   Ⓐ ∠MLN
   Ⓑ ∠KPN
   Ⓒ ∠KLM
   Ⓓ ∠LNP

18. Which is parallel to $\overline{KP}$?

   Ⓕ $\overline{PL}$
   Ⓖ $\overline{LN}$
   Ⓗ $\overline{PM}$
   Ⓙ $\overline{LM}$

Use this map and an inch ruler to answer questions 19 and 20.

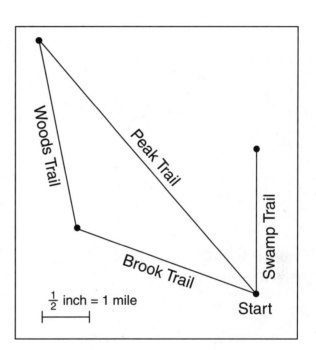

19. What is the actual distance from the START to the end of the Swamp Trail?

   Ⓐ $\frac{3}{4}$ miles   Ⓒ 2 miles

   Ⓑ $1\frac{1}{2}$ miles   Ⓓ 3 miles

20. Jed hiked from the START to the end of the Peak Trail. Then he hiked back on the Woods Trail and the Brook Trail. How far did he hike in all?

   Ⓕ 15 miles   Ⓗ 9 miles

   Ⓖ 12 miles   Ⓙ $7\frac{1}{2}$ miles

GO ON

Practice Test 6 (continued)

21. What is the volume of this figure?

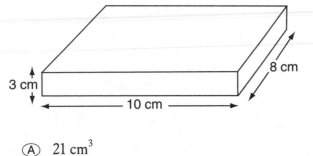

Ⓐ 21 cm³
Ⓑ 80 cm³
Ⓒ 240 cm³
Ⓓ 480 cm³

22. This figure will be turned 180° in the direction shown.

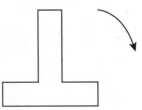

What will the figure look like after it has been turned?

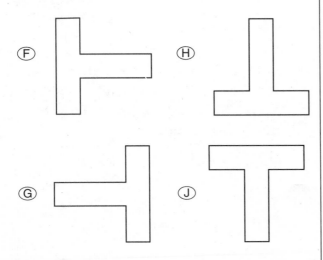

This chart shows the median price of a single-family home in different cities for 1998 and 2000. Use the chart to answer questions 23 and 24.

Price of Home		
City	1998	2000
Baltimore, MD	$120,600	$145,200
Cleveland, OH	121,800	121,300
Kalamazoo, MI	102,300	111,400
Sarasota, FL	123,100	142,000
Tulsa, OK	89,300	93,600

23. What was the median price of a home in Kalamazoo, MI, in 1998?
Ⓐ $102,300
Ⓑ $111,400
Ⓒ $121,800
Ⓓ $123,100

24. From 1998 to 2000, how much did the median price of a home go up in Sarasota, FL?
Ⓕ $4300
Ⓖ $9100
Ⓗ $18,900
Ⓙ $24,600

STOP

ANSWER SHEET

Practice Test # 6

Student Name _____ Grade _____

Teacher Name _____ Date _____

MATHEMATICS

1 Ⓐ Ⓑ Ⓒ Ⓓ Ⓔ	11 Ⓐ Ⓑ Ⓒ Ⓓ Ⓔ	21 Ⓐ Ⓑ Ⓒ Ⓓ Ⓔ	31 Ⓐ Ⓑ Ⓒ Ⓓ Ⓔ
2 Ⓕ Ⓖ Ⓗ Ⓙ Ⓚ	12 Ⓕ Ⓖ Ⓗ Ⓙ Ⓚ	22 Ⓕ Ⓖ Ⓗ Ⓙ Ⓚ	32 Ⓕ Ⓖ Ⓗ Ⓙ Ⓚ
3 Ⓐ Ⓑ Ⓒ Ⓓ Ⓔ	13 Ⓐ Ⓑ Ⓒ Ⓓ Ⓔ	23 Ⓐ Ⓑ Ⓒ Ⓓ Ⓔ	33 Ⓐ Ⓑ Ⓒ Ⓓ Ⓔ
4 Ⓕ Ⓖ Ⓗ Ⓙ Ⓚ	14 Ⓕ Ⓖ Ⓗ Ⓙ Ⓚ	24 Ⓕ Ⓖ Ⓗ Ⓙ Ⓚ	34 Ⓕ Ⓖ Ⓗ Ⓙ Ⓚ
5 Ⓐ Ⓑ Ⓒ Ⓓ Ⓔ	15 Ⓐ Ⓑ Ⓒ Ⓓ Ⓔ	25 Ⓐ Ⓑ Ⓒ Ⓓ Ⓔ	35 Ⓐ Ⓑ Ⓒ Ⓓ Ⓔ
6 Ⓕ Ⓖ Ⓗ Ⓙ Ⓚ	16 Ⓕ Ⓖ Ⓗ Ⓙ Ⓚ	26 Ⓕ Ⓖ Ⓗ Ⓙ Ⓚ	36 Ⓕ Ⓖ Ⓗ Ⓙ Ⓚ
7 Ⓐ Ⓑ Ⓒ Ⓓ Ⓔ	17 Ⓐ Ⓑ Ⓒ Ⓓ Ⓔ	27 Ⓐ Ⓑ Ⓒ Ⓓ Ⓔ	37 Ⓐ Ⓑ Ⓒ Ⓓ Ⓔ
8 Ⓕ Ⓖ Ⓗ Ⓙ Ⓚ	18 Ⓕ Ⓖ Ⓗ Ⓙ Ⓚ	28 Ⓕ Ⓖ Ⓗ Ⓙ Ⓚ	38 Ⓕ Ⓖ Ⓗ Ⓙ Ⓚ
9 Ⓐ Ⓑ Ⓒ Ⓓ Ⓔ	19 Ⓐ Ⓑ Ⓒ Ⓓ Ⓔ	29 Ⓐ Ⓑ Ⓒ Ⓓ Ⓔ	39 Ⓐ Ⓑ Ⓒ Ⓓ Ⓔ
10 Ⓕ Ⓖ Ⓗ Ⓙ Ⓚ	20 Ⓕ Ⓖ Ⓗ Ⓙ Ⓚ	30 Ⓕ Ⓖ Ⓗ Ⓙ Ⓚ	40 Ⓕ Ⓖ Ⓗ Ⓙ Ⓚ

Practice
Test 7
Problem Solving

Name _____   Date _____

Practice Test 7

Directions. Choose the best answer to each question. Mark your answer. If the correct answer is *not given,* choose "NG."

1. In an airplane, there are 32 rows of seats and 6 seats in each row. How many seats are there in all?
- Ⓐ 38
- Ⓑ 182
- Ⓒ 192
- Ⓓ 202
- Ⓔ NG

2. Collin bought these 3 CDs.

$24.95 $16.90 $14.75

What is the total cost of these CDs?
- Ⓕ $56.60
- Ⓖ $54.60
- Ⓗ $41.85
- Ⓙ $39.70
- Ⓚ NG

3. Sela jogged $2\frac{1}{2}$ miles to the lake. Then she jogged $3\frac{3}{4}$ miles on the way back. How far did she jog in all?
- Ⓐ $5\frac{1}{4}$ miles
- Ⓑ $5\frac{1}{2}$ miles
- Ⓒ 6 miles
- Ⓓ $6\frac{1}{2}$ miles
- Ⓔ NG

4. A total of 160 children play in the city soccer league, and 64 of the players are girls. What percent of the players are girls?
- Ⓕ 96%
- Ⓖ 56%
- Ⓗ 40%
- Ⓙ 30%
- Ⓚ NG

5. Boxes of greeting cards cost $7.95 each, or you can buy a set of 3 boxes for $20.00.

$7.95 $20.00

How much do you save on 3 boxes if you buy the set?
- Ⓐ $23.85
- Ⓑ $3.85
- Ⓒ $2.95
- Ⓓ $1.75
- Ⓔ NG

6. A garden store had 25 flats of tomato plants for sale. There were 12 plants in each flat. Customers bought 184 of the plants. How many tomato plants were left?
- Ⓕ 300
- Ⓖ 216
- Ⓗ 196
- Ⓙ 116
- Ⓚ NG

GO ON

Scholastic Professional Books

Practice Test 7 (continued)

7. Caroline wants to buy a scooter that usually costs $105.00. The scooter is on sale.

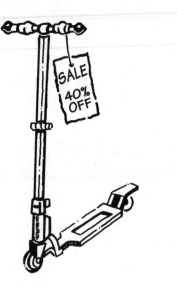

What is the sale price of the scooter?
- Ⓐ $40.00
- Ⓑ $42.00
- Ⓒ $53.00
- Ⓓ $63.00
- Ⓔ NG

8. Jackson started writing a story at 8:30 A.M. He stopped writing at 1:15 P.M. How long did he write?
- Ⓕ 3 hr, 45 min
- Ⓖ 3 hr, 55 min
- Ⓗ 4 hr, 15 min
- Ⓙ 4 hr, 30 min
- Ⓚ NG

9. At the car wash, 6 cars are washed every 15 minutes. At this rate, how long would it take to wash 24 cars?
- Ⓐ 1 hour
- Ⓑ 50 min
- Ⓒ 40 min
- Ⓓ 36 min
- Ⓔ NG

10. On a Saturday morning, there were 84 cars in the parking lot at the bowling alley. Of those cars, $\frac{2}{3}$ were black. How many black cars were in the parking lot?
- Ⓕ 28
- Ⓖ 42
- Ⓗ 56
- Ⓙ 72
- Ⓚ NG

11. Ansley baked 3 dozen cupcakes for a bake sale. If she sold all the cupcakes for $0.75 each, how much money would she collect?
- Ⓐ $48.00
- Ⓑ $32.00
- Ⓒ $27.00
- Ⓓ $22.50
- Ⓔ NG

Scholastic Professional Books

Practice Test 7 *(continued)*

12. Five students stood in line for lunch in the cafeteria. Mandy stood in front of John and behind Gary. Fran stood in front of Gary and behind Claude. Who was first in line?

  Ⓕ Claude
  Ⓖ Fran
  Ⓗ Mandy
  Ⓙ John
  Ⓚ NG

13. There are 31 passenger cars on a train. Each car has 104 seats.

Which numbers would give the best estimate of the total number of seats on this train?

  Ⓐ 30 × 90
  Ⓑ 30 × 100
  Ⓒ 40 × 90
  Ⓓ 40 × 100

14. A paperback book costs $8.95. <u>About</u> how much would 58 of these books cost?

  Ⓕ $400
  Ⓖ $450
  Ⓗ $480
  Ⓙ $540

15. Mrs. Charles rides 12 miles a day on her bike. <u>About</u> how many miles will she ride in 29 days?

  Ⓐ 300
  Ⓑ 500
  Ⓒ 700
  Ⓓ 900

16. For 5 days, Stacey waited on customers at the pet store. She waited on 31 customers on the first day and 40 customers on the second day. What else do you need to know to find the average number of customers she waited on each day?

  Ⓕ the total number of customers in the 5 days
  Ⓖ how many customers she served on the last day
  Ⓗ on which days of the week she worked
  Ⓙ the number of pets she sold in those 5 days

GO ON

Practice Test 7 (continued)

17. Garrett mows lawns for $10 an hour. Last week he earned $140 mowing lawns. Which question can you answer from this information?

Ⓐ How many lawns did Garrett mow?

Ⓑ What is the average amount of money Garrett earns each week?

Ⓒ How many hours did Garrett spend mowing lawns last week?

Ⓓ How much money does Garrett make during the summer?

Ⓔ NG

18. A store owner received 18 cases of soda. Each case has 24 cans of soda. The owner sells each can for $0.60. Which number sentence should you use to find how much money the owner will collect if he sells all the soda?

Ⓕ $(18 \times 24) + \$0.60 = \square$

Ⓖ $(18 \times 24) \times \$0.60 = \square$

Ⓗ $(18 \times 24) \div \$0.60 = \square$

Ⓙ $(18 \times 24) - \$0.60 = \square$

Ⓚ NG

19. Mr. Clemens and his daughter caught 30 fish one day. Of those fish, 18 were flounder. What percent of the fish were flounder?

Ⓐ 30%

Ⓑ 40%

Ⓒ 50%

Ⓓ 70%

Ⓔ NG

20. Janine was making potato salad for a picnic. She used $8\frac{3}{4}$ pounds of russet potatoes and $6\frac{5}{8}$ pounds of Idaho potatoes.

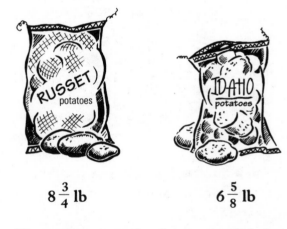

$8\frac{3}{4}$ lb $6\frac{5}{8}$ lb

How many pounds of potatoes did she use in all?

Ⓕ $14\frac{1}{8}$ lb

Ⓖ $14\frac{3}{8}$ lb

Ⓗ $15\frac{1}{8}$ lb

Ⓙ $15\frac{3}{8}$ lb

Ⓚ NG

GO ON ⇨

Practice Test 7 (continued)

21. Ms. Lopis bought 2 pairs of skis at a ski sale.

Including a sales tax of 6%, what was the total cost of the 2 pairs of skis?

Ⓐ $826.80
Ⓑ $790.00
Ⓒ $413.40
Ⓓ $390.00
Ⓔ NG

22. At the movie theater, 102 adults and 60 children went to the five o'clock show. Adults paid $6.50 per ticket. Children's tickets were $4.00 each.

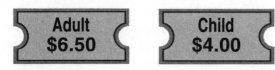

How much money was spent on tickets for the five o'clock show?

Ⓕ $903.00
Ⓖ $863.00
Ⓗ $663.00
Ⓙ $240.00
Ⓚ NG

23. On average, 118 cars go through the toll booth each hour. How many cars go through the toll booth in 8 hours?

Ⓐ 126
Ⓑ 864
Ⓒ 934
Ⓓ 1044
Ⓔ NG

24. A mason can lay 20 bricks in 30 minutes. At this rate, how long will it take him to lay 100 bricks?

Ⓕ 60 minutes
Ⓖ 90 minutes
Ⓗ 120 minutes
Ⓙ 150 minutes
Ⓚ NG

25. In a race, Amy swam 100 meters in 59.13 seconds. Inge's time was 56.61 seconds. How much faster was Inge's time in the race?

Ⓐ 3.52 seconds
Ⓑ 2.81 seconds
Ⓒ 2.74 seconds
Ⓓ 2.52 seconds
Ⓔ NG

Student Name _____   Grade _____

Teacher Name _____   Date _____

MATHEMATICS

1 Ⓐ Ⓑ Ⓒ Ⓓ Ⓔ	11 Ⓐ Ⓑ Ⓒ Ⓓ Ⓔ	21 Ⓐ Ⓑ Ⓒ Ⓓ Ⓔ	31 Ⓐ Ⓑ Ⓒ Ⓓ Ⓔ
2 Ⓕ Ⓖ Ⓗ Ⓙ Ⓚ	12 Ⓕ Ⓖ Ⓗ Ⓙ Ⓚ	22 Ⓕ Ⓖ Ⓗ Ⓙ Ⓚ	32 Ⓕ Ⓖ Ⓗ Ⓙ Ⓚ
3 Ⓐ Ⓑ Ⓒ Ⓓ Ⓔ	13 Ⓐ Ⓑ Ⓒ Ⓓ Ⓔ	23 Ⓐ Ⓑ Ⓒ Ⓓ Ⓔ	33 Ⓐ Ⓑ Ⓒ Ⓓ Ⓔ
4 Ⓕ Ⓖ Ⓗ Ⓙ Ⓚ	14 Ⓕ Ⓖ Ⓗ Ⓙ Ⓚ	24 Ⓕ Ⓖ Ⓗ Ⓙ Ⓚ	34 Ⓕ Ⓖ Ⓗ Ⓙ Ⓚ
5 Ⓐ Ⓑ Ⓒ Ⓓ Ⓔ	15 Ⓐ Ⓑ Ⓒ Ⓓ Ⓔ	25 Ⓐ Ⓑ Ⓒ Ⓓ Ⓔ	35 Ⓐ Ⓑ Ⓒ Ⓓ Ⓔ
6 Ⓕ Ⓖ Ⓗ Ⓙ Ⓚ	16 Ⓕ Ⓖ Ⓗ Ⓙ Ⓚ	26 Ⓕ Ⓖ Ⓗ Ⓙ Ⓚ	36 Ⓕ Ⓖ Ⓗ Ⓙ Ⓚ
7 Ⓐ Ⓑ Ⓒ Ⓓ Ⓔ	17 Ⓐ Ⓑ Ⓒ Ⓓ Ⓔ	27 Ⓐ Ⓑ Ⓒ Ⓓ Ⓔ	37 Ⓐ Ⓑ Ⓒ Ⓓ Ⓔ
8 Ⓕ Ⓖ Ⓗ Ⓙ Ⓚ	18 Ⓕ Ⓖ Ⓗ Ⓙ Ⓚ	28 Ⓕ Ⓖ Ⓗ Ⓙ Ⓚ	38 Ⓕ Ⓖ Ⓗ Ⓙ Ⓚ
9 Ⓐ Ⓑ Ⓒ Ⓓ Ⓔ	19 Ⓐ Ⓑ Ⓒ Ⓓ Ⓔ	29 Ⓐ Ⓑ Ⓒ Ⓓ Ⓔ	39 Ⓐ Ⓑ Ⓒ Ⓓ Ⓔ
10 Ⓕ Ⓖ Ⓗ Ⓙ Ⓚ	20 Ⓕ Ⓖ Ⓗ Ⓙ Ⓚ	30 Ⓕ Ⓖ Ⓗ Ⓙ Ⓚ	40 Ⓕ Ⓖ Ⓗ Ⓙ Ⓚ

Practice
Test 8
Computation

Practice Test 8

Directions. Choose the best answer to each question. Mark your answer. If the correct answer is *not given,* choose "NG."

1. $\begin{array}{r} 65 \\ \times\, 28 \end{array}$

- Ⓐ 650
- Ⓑ 1820
- Ⓒ 1828
- Ⓓ 1920
- Ⓔ NG

2. $7\overline{)212}$

- Ⓕ 30
- Ⓖ 30 R1
- Ⓗ 30 R2
- Ⓙ 31 R2
- Ⓚ NG

3. $35\overline{)490}$

- Ⓐ 14
- Ⓑ 15
- Ⓒ 16
- Ⓓ 17
- Ⓔ NG

4. **This chart shows how many hours Mr. Crane worked each week.**

Hours Worked	
Week 1	42
Week 2	50
Week 3	58
Week 4	48
Week 5	42

What was the average number of hours he worked per week?

- Ⓕ 42 hours
- Ⓖ 48 hours
- Ⓗ 50 hours
- Ⓙ 240 hours
- Ⓚ NG

5. **A passenger ferry can carry 462 passengers.**

462

How many passengers can the ferry carry in 3 trips?

- Ⓐ 924
- Ⓑ 1396
- Ⓒ 1406
- Ⓓ 1848
- Ⓔ NG

GO ON ▷

Practice Test 8 (continued)

6. $\frac{3}{4} + \frac{3}{8} =$

- Ⓕ $\frac{1}{2}$
- Ⓖ $1\frac{1}{4}$
- Ⓗ $\frac{6}{12}$
- Ⓙ $1\frac{1}{8}$
- Ⓚ NG

7. $\frac{1}{6} + \frac{5}{12} =$

- Ⓐ $\frac{6}{18}$
- Ⓑ $\frac{7}{12}$
- Ⓒ $\frac{1}{3}$
- Ⓓ $\frac{5}{7}$
- Ⓔ NG

8. $4\frac{1}{3}$
  $-\ \frac{2}{3}$

- Ⓕ $2\frac{2}{3}$
- Ⓖ 3
- Ⓗ $3\frac{1}{3}$
- Ⓙ 4
- Ⓚ NG

9. $\frac{1}{4} \times \frac{4}{5} =$

- Ⓐ $\frac{3}{20}$
- Ⓑ $\frac{4}{9}$
- Ⓒ $\frac{3}{10}$
- Ⓓ $\frac{1}{5}$
- Ⓔ NG

10. Greg has 2 different bike helmets, 6 shirts, and 3 pairs of bike shorts.

Biking Gear		
Helmets	Shirts	Shorts
2	6	3

How many different combinations of 1 helmet, 1 shirt, and 1 pair of shorts can he make?

- Ⓕ 11
- Ⓖ 24
- Ⓗ 36
- Ⓙ 48
- Ⓚ NG

11. Melanie played a fishing game at the fair. These colored fish were in the fish tank.

Color	Number of Fish
Red	25
Green	30
White	25
Blue	20

If Melanie catches one fish without looking, what is the probability that the fish will be blue?

- Ⓐ $\frac{1}{3}$
- Ⓑ $\frac{1}{4}$
- Ⓒ $\frac{1}{5}$
- Ⓓ $\frac{1}{6}$
- Ⓔ NG

GO ON

Practice Test 8 (continued)

12. $148.25
      + 79.80

   Ⓕ $68.45
   Ⓖ $227.05
   Ⓗ $227.65
   Ⓙ $228.05
   Ⓚ NG

Use the graph below to answer questions 16 and 17.

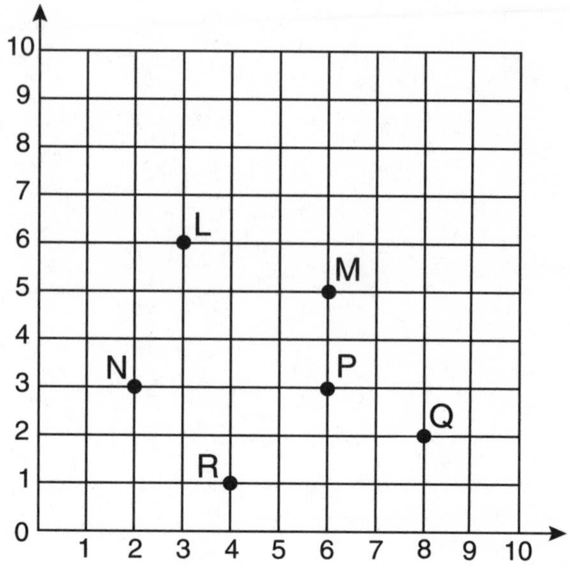

13. 61.05
      − 38.29

   Ⓐ 99.34
   Ⓑ 37.26
   Ⓒ 22.76
   Ⓓ 21.86
   Ⓔ NG

14. $4 \times 0.9 =$

   Ⓕ 360
   Ⓖ 36
   Ⓗ 3.6
   Ⓙ 0.36
   Ⓚ NG

16. Where is point Q located?
   Ⓕ (4, 1)
   Ⓖ (2, 8)
   Ⓗ (3, 6)
   Ⓙ (8, 2)
   Ⓚ NG

15. $6\overline{)48.3}$

   Ⓐ 8.5
   Ⓑ 8.05
   Ⓒ 7.5
   Ⓓ 7.05
   Ⓔ NG

17. What point is located at (6, 5)?
   Ⓐ point M
   Ⓑ point N
   Ⓒ point P
   Ⓓ point R
   Ⓔ NG

GO ON

Practice Test 8 (continued)

18. 12% of 50 =

Ⓕ 5
Ⓖ 6
Ⓗ 38
Ⓙ 60
Ⓚ NG

19. 80% of $60 =

Ⓐ $14
Ⓑ $30
Ⓒ $40
Ⓓ $42
Ⓔ NG

20. 15 is what percent of 30?

Ⓕ 15%
Ⓖ 30%
Ⓗ 45%
Ⓙ 50%
Ⓚ NG

21. $-15 + 8 =$

Ⓐ 23
Ⓑ –8
Ⓒ 7
Ⓓ –7
Ⓔ NG

22. This table shows the number of children who went to Pinehurst School each year.

| Children at Pinehurst School ||
Year	Number of Children
1998	160
1999	240
2000	300
2001	280

What was the average number of children who went to the school each year?

Ⓕ 245
Ⓖ 280
Ⓗ 490
Ⓙ 980
Ⓚ NG

23. This table lists the scores Merrill got on 5 spelling tests.

Test	Score
1	65
2	90
3	84
4	78
5	82

What was Merrill's median test score?

Ⓐ 65
Ⓑ 78
Ⓒ 82
Ⓓ 84
Ⓔ NG

GO ON

Scholastic Professional Books

Practice Test 8 *(continued)*

24. If $5x - 4 = 31$, what is the value of x?

    Ⓕ 6

    Ⓖ 7

    Ⓗ 8

    Ⓙ 10

    Ⓚ NG

25. If $3n + 8 = 44$, what is the value of n?

    Ⓐ 6

    Ⓑ 8

    Ⓒ 10

    Ⓓ 12

    Ⓔ NG

26. If $6y > 24$, what is the value of y?

    Ⓕ $y < 3$

    Ⓖ $y < 4$

    Ⓗ $y > 3$

    Ⓙ $y > 4$

    Ⓚ NG

27. At 4:00 A.M., the temperature was 30°F. This table shows how much the temperature changed during the day.

Time	Change in Temperature (°F)
10:00 A.M.	−6
2:00 P.M.	+4
6:00 P.M.	−2
10:00 P.M.	−5

What was the temperature at 10:00 P.M.?

    Ⓐ 21°F

    Ⓑ 32°F

    Ⓒ 35°F

    Ⓓ 47°F

    Ⓔ NG

28. A bean plant grew $1\frac{1}{2}$ inches per day. How much did the plant grow in 9 days?

    Ⓕ $10\frac{1}{2}$ in.

    Ⓖ 12 in.

    Ⓗ $13\frac{1}{2}$ in.

    Ⓙ 15 in.

    Ⓚ NG

Scholastic Professional Books

ANSWER SHEET

Student Name _____ Grade _____

Teacher Name _____ Date _____

MATHEMATICS

1 Ⓐ Ⓑ Ⓒ Ⓓ Ⓔ	11 Ⓐ Ⓑ Ⓒ Ⓓ Ⓔ	21 Ⓐ Ⓑ Ⓒ Ⓓ Ⓔ	31 Ⓐ Ⓑ Ⓒ Ⓓ Ⓔ
2 Ⓕ Ⓖ Ⓗ Ⓙ Ⓚ	12 Ⓕ Ⓖ Ⓗ Ⓙ Ⓚ	22 Ⓕ Ⓖ Ⓗ Ⓙ Ⓚ	32 Ⓕ Ⓖ Ⓗ Ⓙ Ⓚ
3 Ⓐ Ⓑ Ⓒ Ⓓ Ⓔ	13 Ⓐ Ⓑ Ⓒ Ⓓ Ⓔ	23 Ⓐ Ⓑ Ⓒ Ⓓ Ⓔ	33 Ⓐ Ⓑ Ⓒ Ⓓ Ⓔ
4 Ⓕ Ⓖ Ⓗ Ⓙ Ⓚ	14 Ⓕ Ⓖ Ⓗ Ⓙ Ⓚ	24 Ⓕ Ⓖ Ⓗ Ⓙ Ⓚ	34 Ⓕ Ⓖ Ⓗ Ⓙ Ⓚ
5 Ⓐ Ⓑ Ⓒ Ⓓ Ⓔ	15 Ⓐ Ⓑ Ⓒ Ⓓ Ⓔ	25 Ⓐ Ⓑ Ⓒ Ⓓ Ⓔ	35 Ⓐ Ⓑ Ⓒ Ⓓ Ⓔ
6 Ⓕ Ⓖ Ⓗ Ⓙ Ⓚ	16 Ⓕ Ⓖ Ⓗ Ⓙ Ⓚ	26 Ⓕ Ⓖ Ⓗ Ⓙ Ⓚ	36 Ⓕ Ⓖ Ⓗ Ⓙ Ⓚ
7 Ⓐ Ⓑ Ⓒ Ⓓ Ⓔ	17 Ⓐ Ⓑ Ⓒ Ⓓ Ⓔ	27 Ⓐ Ⓑ Ⓒ Ⓓ Ⓔ	37 Ⓐ Ⓑ Ⓒ Ⓓ Ⓔ
8 Ⓕ Ⓖ Ⓗ Ⓙ Ⓚ	18 Ⓕ Ⓖ Ⓗ Ⓙ Ⓚ	28 Ⓕ Ⓖ Ⓗ Ⓙ Ⓚ	38 Ⓕ Ⓖ Ⓗ Ⓙ Ⓚ
9 Ⓐ Ⓑ Ⓒ Ⓓ Ⓔ	19 Ⓐ Ⓑ Ⓒ Ⓓ Ⓔ	29 Ⓐ Ⓑ Ⓒ Ⓓ Ⓔ	39 Ⓐ Ⓑ Ⓒ Ⓓ Ⓔ
10 Ⓕ Ⓖ Ⓗ Ⓙ Ⓚ	20 Ⓕ Ⓖ Ⓗ Ⓙ Ⓚ	30 Ⓕ Ⓖ Ⓗ Ⓙ Ⓚ	40 Ⓕ Ⓖ Ⓗ Ⓙ Ⓚ

Scholastic Professional Books

Practice Test 1   Tested Skills

Tested Skills	Item Numbers
Numeration and Number Concepts	
Associate numerals and number words	1, 2
Compare and order whole numbers and integers	3, 4, 5
Use place value and rounding	6, 8, 9
Use exponents and expanded forms	10, 11, 12
Identify patterns	7, 13, 14
Identify prime numbers, factors, and multiples	15, 16, 17
Estimation	18, 19
Use a number line	20, 24
Identify fractional parts	21, 22
Compare and order fractions and decimals	23, 25
Rename fractions, decimals, and percents	26, 27
Apply operational properties	28

Practice Test 2   Tested Skills

Tested Skills	Item Numbers
Geometry and Measurement	
Identify parts and characteristics of plane and solid figures	1, 3, 5, 6
Recognize symmetry and congruence	7, 8
Identify points, lines, line segments, and angles	17, 18
Identify transformations	22
Find perimeter, circumference, area, and volume	4, 11, 21
Use appropriate units of measurement	10, 16
Convert units of measure (standard, metric)	2, 9
Estimate measurements	12, 13
Use scale to determine distance	19, 20
Interpret graphs, charts, and tables	14, 15, 23, 24

Practice Test 3   Tested Skills

Tested Skills	Item Numbers
Problem Solving	
Solve problems involving basic operations	1, 3, 10, 23
Solve problems involving money, time, and measurement	2, 8, 11, 20, 25
Solve problems involving percents and discount	4, 7, 19
Use estimation to solve problems	13, 14, 15
Solve problems involving ratio, proportion, and logic	9, 12, 24
Identify steps in solving problems	16, 17, 18
Solve multi-step problems	5, 6, 21, 22

Practice Test 4   Tested Skills

Tested Skills	Item Numbers
Computation, Statistics, and Algebra	
Compute with whole numbers	1, 2, 3, 5
Compute with fractions and mixed numbers	6, 7, 8, 9, 28
Compute with decimals	12, 13, 14, 15
Find percents	18, 19, 20
Complete operations with integers	21, 27
Find average, median, probability, and combinations	4, 10, 11, 22, 23
Solve simple equations and inequalities	24, 25, 26
Find/plot points on a coordinate graph	16, 17

Practice Test 5   Tested Skills

Numeration and Number Concepts	Item Numbers
Associate numerals and number words	1, 2
Compare and order whole numbers and integers	3, 4, 5
Use place value and rounding	6, 8, 9
Use exponents and expanded forms	10, 11, 12
Identify patterns	7, 13, 14
Identify prime numbers, factors, and multiples	15, 16, 17
Estimation	18, 19
Use a number line	20, 24
Identify fractional parts	21, 22
Compare and order fractions and decimals	23, 25
Rename fractions, decimals, and percents	26, 27
Apply operational properties	28

Practice Test 6   Tested Skills

Geometry and Measurement	Item Numbers
Identify parts and characteristics of plane and solid figures	1, 3, 5, 6
Recognize symmetry and congruence	7, 8
Identify points, lines, line segments, and angles	17, 18
Identify transformations	22
Find perimeter, circumference, area, and volume	4, 11, 21
Use appropriate units of measurement	10, 16
Convert units of measure (standard, metric)	2, 9
Estimate measurements	12, 13
Use scale to determine distance	19, 20
Interpret graphs, charts, and tables	14, 15, 23, 24

Practice Test 7   Tested Skills

Problem Solving	Item Numbers
Solve problems involving basic operations	1, 3, 10, 23
Solve problems involving money, time, and measurement	2, 8, 11, 20, 25
Solve problems involving percents and discount	4, 7, 19
Use estimation to solve problems	13, 14, 15
Solve problems involving ratio, proportion, and logic	9, 12, 24
Identify steps in solving problems	16, 17, 18
Solve multi-step problems	5, 6, 21, 22

Practice Test 8   Tested Skills

Computation, Statistics, and Algebra	Item Numbers
Compute with whole numbers	1, 2, 3, 5
Compute with fractions and mixed numbers	6, 7, 8, 9, 28
Compute with decimals	12, 13, 14, 15
Find percents	18, 19, 20
Complete operations with integers	21, 27
Find average, median, probability, and combinations	4, 10, 11, 22, 23
Solve simple equations and inequalities	24, 25, 26
Find/plot points on a coordinate graph	16, 17

ANSWER KEY

Practice Test 1

Numeration and Number Concepts

1. B	15. D
2. H	16. G
3. D	17. B
4. F	18. H
5. A	19. A
6. F	20. G
7. C	21. B
8. G	22. F
9. D	23. B
10. H	24. H
11. B	25. D
12. J	26. F
13. C	27. C
14. F	28. G

Practice Test 2

Geometry and Measurement

1. C	13. B
2. G	14. J
3. A	15. D
4. J	16. F
5. D	17. D
6. F	18. G
7. B	19. B
8. G	20. J
9. D	21. A
10. H	22. H
11. C	23. B
12. H	24. J

Practice Test 3

Problem Solving

1. B	14. H
2. J	15. B
3. C	16. F
4. G	17. D
5. A	18. G
6. H	19. E
7. C	20. H
8. K	21. A
9. D	22. J
10. H	23. C
11. E	24. K
12. J	25. B
13. C	

Practice Test 4

Computation

1. C	15. C
2. G	16. F
3. E	17. D
4. H	18. G
5. D	19. E
6. F	20. J
7. D	21. A
8. K	22. F
9. C	23. B
10. J	24. F
11. B	25. D
12. J	26. H
13. E	27. C
14. G	28. J

Practice Test 5

Numeration and Number Concepts

1. C	15. C
2. F	16. G
3. A	17. B
4. H	18. G
5. D	19. C
6. G	20. J
7. B	21. A
8. J	22. F
9. C	23. B
10. F	24. H
11. C	25. C
12. G	26. F
13. D	27. B
14. J	28. J

Practice Test 6

Geometry and Measurement

1. D	13. C
2. F	14. J
3. B	15. B
4. H	16. H
5. A	17. A
6. J	18. G
7. B	19. D
8. G	20. F
9. A	21. C
10. H	22. J
11. D	23. A
12. H	24. H

Practice Test 7

Problem Solving

1. C	14. J
2. F	15. A
3. E	16. F
4. H	17. C
5. B	18. G
6. J	19. E
7. D	20. J
8. K	21. A
9. A	22. F
10. H	23. E
11. C	24. J
12. F	25. D
13. B	

Practice Test 8

Computation

1. B	15. B
2. H	16. J
3. A	17. A
4. G	18. G
5. E	19. E
6. J	20. J
7. B	21. D
8. K	22. F
9. D	23. C
10. H	24. G
11. C	25. D
12. J	26. J
13. C	27. A
14. H	28. H